TIMELESS PLACES

THE GREEK ISLES

LAURA BROOKS

MetroBooks

MetroBooks

An Imprint of the Michael Friedman Publishing Group, Inc.

©2000 by Michael Friedman Publishing Group, Inc.
First MetroBooks Edition 2002

Library of Congress Cataloging-in-Publication Data

Brooks, Laura.
    Greek Isles / Laura Brooks.
        p. cm. — (Timeless places)
    Includes index.
    ISBN 1-58663-879-3 (alk. paper)
    1. Islands—greece—Pictorial works. 2. Islands—Greece—History. I. Title. II. Series.

DF261 .B76 2000
949.5'00942—dc21

00-039340

Editors: Ann Kirby-Payne and Alexandra Bonfante-Warren
Art Director: Jeff Batzli
Designer: Jennifer S. Markson
Photography Editor: Wendy Missan
Production Manager: Maria Gonzalez

Color separations by Colourscan Overseas
Printed in Hong Kong by Midas Printing Limited

1 3 5 7 9 10 8 6 4 2

For bulk purchases and special sales, please contact:
Michael Friedman Publishing Group, Inc.
Attention: Sales Department
230 Fifth Avenue
New York, NY 10001
212/685-6610 FAX 212/685-3916

Visit our website:
www.metrobooks.com

❉

PAGE 1: **Large pelicans are a common sight throughout the Greek Isles. On Mykonos, this friendly creature has become a mascot.**

PAGES 2–3: **As dusk falls on Santorini, a thousand lights twinkle against the stark white geometric architecture. People wait until the hot sun recedes to enjoy the evening breezes with a stroll. Some will dine, some will dance and make merry in local *tavernas*.**

PAGES 4–5: **The church of Panagia Paraportiani on the island of Mykonos raises its age-softened lines to sun.**

PAGE 6: **Near Lalaria Beach, on Skiathos, translucent waters swirl peacefully around craggy outcrops of rocky shoreline. The sun paints pictures on a shifting sea.**

Contents

※

PAGE 7: **A fisherman on Sikinos rises before dawn to prepare his boat for a day at sea—a ritual that has played out every morning for thousands of years.**

RIGHT: **Each holiday has its special baked treats. Here, women in traditional dress prepare a delectable bread made only at Easter.**

PAGES 10–11: **Constant breezes blow across the hills of the Greek Isles, powering ancient windmills that have ground grain for centuries. By the fourteenth century, the great number of windmills in the harbor of Rhodes earned it the name Harbor of Windmills.**

PART I

HISTORY

Its face is an inverted triangle, its nose a sloping plane of stone, its body a minimalistic suggestion etched into marble. At first glance, you might think that this masterpiece of abstraction was sculpted by a leading artist of the twentieth century. Look again. This idol was carved on a tiny island in the Aegean Sea nearly four thousand years ago. This elegant human figure was never destined for a modern museum but, rather, was offered to the gods on an ancient altar.

The contradiction embodied in this object—an ancient sculpture that seems entirely contemporary to the twenty-first-century viewer—captures the essence of the Greek Isles. These islands form a backdrop for a culture that transcends time. Life follows its own rhythm on these gems of the sea that spread east from the Greek mainland. For eons, the artisans of the region have crafted beautiful objects of marble, bronze, and wood. For centuries, mules have transported people and goods from bustling port towns to the traditional villages that dot the hillsides. Ancient windmills—perched above glistening harbors like stalwart sentries—have harnessed the power of the air to process grain for as long as anyone can remember. Every day for thousands of years, fishermen have launched their boats in search of those fruits of the sea so lavishly displayed in seaside markets. Islanders have flocked to natural hot springs to bask in their healing waters since before the time of Aristotle. And since long before that, shrines to the gods have lured pilgrims and worshipers from near and far.

❈

OPPOSITE: **Standing in the silence of centuries, ancient ruins on the island of Kos attest to the rich heritage of classical culture throughout the Greek Isles.**

It is no wonder that historians trace the birth of Western civilization to these jewels of the Aegean, Ionian, and Mediterranean seas. The Greek Isles are home to wide-ranging and far-reaching cultural traditions and mythic tales, not to mention the colorful history and unforgettable vistas that still draw thousands of tourists to the region every year. Minoan ruins stand alongside Byzantine churches and Crusader fortresses. Terra-cotta pots spilling over with hibiscus flowers adorn blinding-white stucco houses that reflect the sun's dazzling light. Fishing villages perched upon craggy cliffs overlook clusters of colorful boats in island harbors. Centuries-old citrus and olive groves dot the hillsides. Lush vegetation and rocky shores meet isolated stretches of sand and an azure sea. Masts bob left and right on sailboats moored in secluded inlets.

Each island is a world unto itself. Although outsiders and neighbors have inhabited, visited, and invaded these islands throughout the centuries, the islands' rugged geography and small size have also ensured a certain isolation. In this environment, traditional ways of life thrive. The arts—pottery, glass blowing, gem carving, sculpture, and painting, among others—flourish here today, as contemporary craft artists keep alive techniques begun in antiquity. In the remote hilltop villages of Kárpathos, for example, artisans practice crafts that date back eons, and inhabitants speak a dialect close to ancient Greek.

Today, to walk along the pebbled pathways of a traditional Greek mountain village or the marbled streets of an ancient acropolis is to step back in time. To meander at a leisurely pace through these island chains by boat is to be captivated by the same dramatic landscapes and enchanted islets that make the myths of ancient Greece so compelling. To witness the Mediterranean sun setting on the turquoise sea is to receive one of life's greatest blessings.

Ancient Ways

Considering their favorable strategic location, pleasant climate, and natural beauty, is it any wonder that the Greek Isles became the cradle of Western culture? For millennia, the Greek islands have exerted a powerful magnetic force on

ABOVE: **Severe and transcendent—the Cycladic art of the third and second millennia B.C.E. is unique. It would be nearly four thousand years before sculptors revived the deft abstraction and elegant proportions of these mysterious figures.**

people around the world. Seafaring conquerors have long recognized the importance and beauty of these islands. Ancient Phoenician ships came ashore as early as the third millennium B.C.E., followed by would-be conquerors from mainland Greece, Rome, Venice, and Turkey. Invaders have laid claim to these islands from antiquity well into the modern era.

Pleasure seekers have also been drawn to the area. Ancient Minoan kings built their luxurious palaces among the citrus groves and rugged hillsides that overlook the placid seas. Scenes depicted in ancient wall paintings and on decorated pottery suggest that the islands have been a center of hedonistic activity—dancing, drinking, and romance—for eons. Today, visitors from around the world indulge in these same activities, drawn to the beaches, *tavernas*, and discotheques that pepper the many island harbors.

Contemporary travelers to the Greek Isles come for myriad reasons and find a dazzling array of unexpected delights, for each of the more than three thousand islands has its own particular character. From the larger, bustling islands of Crete, Rhodes, and the island nation of Cyprus to the quieter havens of Folegandros and Kárpathos, to the hundreds of tiny, uninhabited islets of the region, the Greek Isles present a collage of diverse landscapes and customs. Mykonos is fun-loving, with lively tavernas and populated beaches. Delos is stoic, protecting the ruins of its ancient sanctuaries in solemn dignity. Milos is magical, with its volcanic rock formations and stunning village vistas.

The Greek Isles are divided into several major chains lying in the Aegean, the Mediterranean, and the Ionian seas. The Cyclades chain alone includes more than two hundred islands clustered in the southern Aegean. In the southeastern Aegean, between Crete and Asia Minor, there are 163 islands known as the Dodecanese chain. Only 26 of these are inhabited; the largest of them is Rhodes, where the world-famous Colossus once stood. The Ionian chain of western Greece (named for the eponymous sea) includes the large island of Corfu. Cyprus lies in the eastern Mediterranean, south of Turkey. Today, Cyprus stands politically divided, with Turkish rule in the north, and a government in the south that remains independent from Greece.

ABOVE: **On Kárpathos, in the Dodecanese island chain, the people perpetuate customs they learned from their own parents and grandparents. Embroidery is one of the most enduring of these. Here, escaping the heat of the afternoon sun, women carefully stitch age-old designs.**

However, the island has always been linked culturally and linguistically to Greece, and it shares traditions and ways of life with the smaller islands scattered to its south and west.

In the Greek Isles, history blends myth and fact. Historians glean information about the early days of the Greek Isles from the countless ancient stories and legends set there. According to Homer, battleships sailed from the harbors of Kos and Rhodes during the Trojan War. A well-known legend holds that the Argonauts sought refuge from a storm on the island of Anafi in the southeastern Cyclades. The lovely island of Lésvos is men-

ABOVE: **The sea carves caves and caverns into the landscape of the Greek Isles. Here, on the island of Zakinthos, clear blue waters rush into the mouth of a gaping cavern.**

tioned throughout the Homeric epics and in many ancient Greek tales. Tradition has it that the god Helios witnessed the island of Rhodes rising mystically from the sea, and chose it for his home. The ill-fated Daedalus and his son, Icarus, attempted to soar through the skies over the magical island of Crete, where the great god Zeus was born in a mountaintop cave. Villagers still recount how Aphrodite emerged from the sea on a breathtaking stretch of beach near the village of Paphos on Cyprus. Visitors must actually lay eyes on a Greek island to gain a full appreciation for these ancient stories. Just setting foot on one of these islands makes you feel as if you've stepped into one of the timeless tales from ancient Greek mythology.

Birthplace of the gods or not, the Greek Isles were home to one of Earth's most ancient civilizations. By the third millennium B.C.E., the so-called Cycladic culture was already flourishing in the islands for which it is named; relics of this society can still be found there. These Bronze Age peoples left no written records, but archaeological discoveries suggest that this well-established civilization possessed a fully developed system of agriculture and a rich religious life. Similar finds on Amorgos and other nearby islands attest to the great importance of this civilization in prehistoric times.

According to some theories, the legendary Atlantis, said to have sunk beneath the sea in a great cataclysm, is in actuality the Greek island of Santorini, which sank partially during the eruption of a volcano around 3500 B.C.E. In any case, by the second millennium B.C.E., the Greek Isles already boasted flourishing commercial towns. Major centers displayed all the trappings of civilized living that characterized the ancient world, from monumental architecture in stone to well-organized trade and political systems. On the larger islands, such as Rhodes and Cyprus, there was often more than one prosperous, bustling town. Because of their strategic locations, some towns became major maritime centers.

From about 3000 B.C.E. to about 1400 B.C.E., the ancient peoples of the Aegean—the Minoans, as they were known—flourished along with their contemporaries, the ancient Egyptians and Mesopotamians, before they perished in a mysterious catastrophe that may have been a volcanic eruption. The Minoans developed written languages, now known as Linear A and Linear B; only the second has been deciphered. Though the Minoan culture has not yielded all of its secrets to contemporary researchers, the spectacular ruins of the palace at Knossos suggest a rich, artistic, and political society. If we are to judge from the fantastic frescoes at Knossos—depicting dancing, general frolicking, and scenes of Minoan hospitality—the ancient Minoans had much in common with the fun-loving modern inhabitants of the Greek Isles.

During the third and second centuries B.C.E., some of the Greek Isles developed cultural centers that rivaled Athens. On Rhodes—a major cultural hub—local sculptors carved the famous Laocoön Group, a masterpiece that depicts a moment from the Odyssey: the death of the Trojan priest Laocoön and his two sons after the priest warned the Trojans against the Greeks' wooden horse. The famous Colossus of Rhodes—a gigantic bronze statue and one of the Seven Wonders of the ancient world—bestrode the entrance to that harbor in 282 B.C.E. Pliny the Elder described it as a marvel, even though it lay on the ground after being toppled by an earthquake just fifty-six years after it was completed. Throughout the islands, the level of cultural activity was matched only by the fervor of commerce, as merchant ships bound for ports throughout the Mediterranean carried pottery, bronze, iron, and other goods from one bustling island harbor to the next.

Temples, city squares, baths, and other ruins attest to a rich civic life in antiquity. In the ancient world, these ports must have teemed with wealthy merchants, petty hawkers, fishermen, locals, and visitors. Vessels with scores of strong-backed rowers rested at port, while the sails of other ships could be sighted off the coast. Villagers and farmers gazed down at the ports from their olive and citrus groves, situated in the remote mountains. Boats laden with perfume, gold, pottery, fabrics, grains, minerals, and slaves sailed to coastal metropolises around the Mediterranean. Traders sailed from port to port bearing wares, and certain islands became famous for specialty products—Thásos, for instance, was known for its marble and gold. Visitors to the larger islands, such as Rhodes, mar-

veled at magnificent marble streets and imposing architecture—majestic temples, shady stoas, and elegant villas—often enclosed within imposing fortifications.

Christianity began to spread through the Mediterranean, and it is believed that Saint John the Evangelist wrote the Book of Revelation—also called the Apocalypse—during his exile from Rome on the island of Patmos. The Monastery of Saint John, built on one of Patmos' highest points, commemorates the work of this biblical scribe. The Greek Isles were part of the Byzantine Empire from the late fourth century onward, and the Christian government promoted the construction of countless houses of worship throughout the islands and on the Greek mainland. In the centuries that followed, Orthodox churches, bejeweled with mosaics and icons, sprang up across the region by the thousands. Throughout the medieval period, European Crusaders used various Greek islands as staging areas for campaigns on the Asian mainland, including attacks on Jerusalem itself. The Knights of Saint John of Jerusalem, also called the Hospitalers, built a stronghold on

ABOVE: **Every morning, Greek fishermen set out from small, sheltered harbors in search of delicious fruits of the sea, including shellfish, squid, and octopi.**

Rhodes and smaller outposts on islands such as Halki. They ruled numerous Greek islands, including Kos, during the thirteenth and fourteenth centuries.

Beginning in the thirteenth and fourteenth centuries, warriors sailed for the Greek Isles from Venice and Genoa. The many fortresses and castles dominating the ports and hilltops of islands such as Zakinthos attest to the military and political aspirations of these medieval conquerors. The mysterious Venetian fortress of Fragokastello on Crete is even said to be inhabited by the ghosts of these invaders. Turkish rulers occupied many islands from the sixteenth century through the twentieth, and mosques replaced some of the churches throughout the islands. Some islands were not united politically with Greece until the middle of the twentieth century, though cultural ties had linked them for many centuries.

What is it about the Greek character that has allowed this complex culture to thrive for millennia? The Greek Isles are home to an enduring, persevering people with a strong work ethic. Proud, patriotic, devout, and insular, these hardy seafarers are the inheritors of working methods that are centuries old. On any given day, fishermen launch their boats at dawn in search of octopi, cuttlefish, sponges, and other gifts of the ocean. Widows clad in black dresses and veils shop the local produce markets and gather in groups of two and three to share stories. Artisans stitch decorative embroidery to adorn traditional costumes. Glassblowers, goldsmiths, and potters continue the work of their ancient ancestors, ultimately displaying their wares in shops along the waterfronts.

The Greeks' dedication to time-honored occupations and hard work is harmoniously complemented by their love of dance, song, food, and games. Some of the earliest works of art from the Greek Isles—including Minoan paintings from the second millennium B.C.E.—depict the central, day-to-day role of dance, and music. Today, life is still lived in common, and the old ways often survive in a deep separation between the worlds of women and men. In the more rural areas, dancing and drinking are—officially at least—reserved for men, as the women watch from windows and doorways before returning to their tasks. At seaside tavernas throughout the

ABOVE: **On Lésvos, in the northeast Aegean Sea, the daily catch is displayed along rocky beaches.**

Greek Isles, old men sip *raki*, a popular aniseed-flavored liqueur, while playing cards or backgammon under grape pergolas that in late summer are heavy with ripe fruit.

Woven into this love of pleasure, however, are strands of superstition and circumspection. For centuries, Greek artisans have crafted the lovely blue and black glass "eyes" that many wear as amulets to ward off evil spirits. They are given as baby and housewarming gifts, and are thought to bring good luck and protect their wearers from the evil eye. Many Greeks carry loops of wooden or glass beads—so-called "worry beads"—for the same purpose. Elderly women take pride in their ability to tell fortunes from the black grounds left behind in a cup of coffee.

Ritual characterizes every aspect of life here, and even mundane, daily activities take on an ageless quality. The daily rhythm begins at dawn, as the fishermen launch boats from countless harbors, an event that has taken place for centuries. The women go to market, exchanging greetings and comments. Ritual rules the care and time taken with every detail of the midday meal, from the hearty seafood appetizers to the strong, syrupy coffee that marks the end of the feast. The day winds down with the evening stroll, a tradition thoroughly ingrained in the culture of

ABOVE: **On Kárpathos, women don local costumes representing centuries of tradition. The styles of the embroidery and jewelry are characteristic of the island.**

the Greek Isles. In villages and towns throughout the islands, sunset brings cooler air and draws people from their homes and the beaches for an enjoyable evening walk through town squares, portside promenades, and narrow streets.

Ancient crafts still flourish in the artisans' studios and in tidy homes of countless mountain villages and ports. Embroidery—traditionally the province of Greek women—is created by hand to adorn the regional costumes worn during festivals. Artists craft delicate silver utensils, engraved gems, blown glass, and gold jewelry. Potters create ceramic pieces featuring some of the same decorative patterns and mythological subjects that captured their ancestors' imagination.

Weddings, festivals, saints' days, and other celebrations with family and friends provide a backdrop for grave and energetic Greek dancing. For centuries—probably ever since people have lived on the islands—Greek islanders have seized every opportunity to play music, sing, and dance. Dancing in Greece is always a group activity, a way to create and reinforce bonds among families, friends, and communities, and island men have been dancing circle dances like the *Kalamatianos* and the *Tsamikos* since antiquity. Musicians accompany revelers on stringed instruments like the bouzouki—the modern equivalents of the lyre.

While traditional attire is reserved mainly for festive occasions, on some islands people still sport these garments daily. On Lefkada and Crete, it is not unusual to find men wearing *vraka*, or baggy trousers, and vests, along with the high boots known as *stivania*. Women wear long, dark, pleated skirts woven on a traditional loom, and long silk scarves or kerchiefs adorn their heads. All the garments are ornamented by hand with rich brocades and elaborate embroidery. All over the Greek Isles, Orthodox priests dress in long black robes, their shadowy figures contrasting with the bright whites, blues, and greens of Greek village architecture.

For centuries, religion has provided an important framework for the rituals and cultural norms that characterize the Greek Isles. Churches and monasteries can be found on every corner of every village and town. For example, the town of Chora on Astypalaia—an island in the Dodecanese—boasts more than three hundred churches and monasteries. Orthodox priests, clad in black from head to toe, preside over their churches, each of which is a brilliant jewelbox of icons and mosaics glittering in the light of a thousand candles. The immutable faces of a hundred saints stare from their gold backgrounds on icons that adorn the altar pieces and the screens that separate the sacred space between priests and the congregation. On feast days, the clergy parade religious icons through streets and pathways lined with reverent onlookers. It is no wonder that Doménikos Theotokópoulos—known to the world as El Greco—emerged from his native Crete as one of the sixteenth century's most intense painters of religious subjects.

On the Greek Isles, Olympian temples gave gracious way to Christian churches. In fact, many churches of the early Byzantine era replaced existing structures dedicated to pre-Christian gods. On Amorgós, the Church of Our Lady in the harbor town of Katápola was built on the site of a former temple of Apollo. Similarly, on Ios, a Byzantine church rose from the ruins of an ancient temple. Mosaic makers, once engaged by prosperous merchants to create lavish pavements for ancient villas and temples, passed their craft down to Byzantine artists who adorned the interiors of their churches with glistening tesserae of multicolored glass, pebbles, pottery shards, and gems. This vibrant chromatic sense also extends to the exterior: the colorful blue, white, or red domes of the Byzantine churches can be seen for miles.

Flourishing for centuries, the thousands of Byzantine churches and monasteries on the Greek Isles bear witness to the depth of the Orthodox tradition and of the medieval culture that once flourished here. On the island of Tínos, for instance, a miraculous icon draws scores of pilgrims and visitors each year to the richly ornamented church of Panagia Evangalestria. For monks seeking retreat from the world and isolation in Edenic surroundings, the Greek Isles seemed the perfect location. Some orders constructed beautiful monasteries from the ground up: on Amorgós, for instance, the historic monastery of Panagia Chozoviotissa, built into the sheer wall of a cliff, stands stark and white against a backdrop of craggy stone. Other monasteries incorporated caves into their complex of chambers and other interior spaces. The cliffsides and remote interiors of many islands are home to still-active Orthodox monasteries, preserving centuries-old practices and countless works of art and objects of worship.

Religious structures represent just one facet of the precious art and architectural heritage of the Greek Isles, where splendid built sites vie with natural wonders for spectacular beauty and interest. Kárpathos and Kíthnos boast rows of picturesque windmills along a rugged coastline. On Santorini, whitewashed villas cling to precipitous cliffs, rising above a turquoise sea. Classical and earlier ruins are eerie reminders of the past on the now-uninhabited island of Delos, which, along with Athens, Olympia, and Delphi, was one of the most important sanctuaries of the ancient world.

Even utilitarian architecture is a feast for the eyes. Stark-white stucco houses with bright blue doors stand silhouetted against the sapphire sea. These white houses look like studies in geometry, their smooth planes and sharp angles reflecting the sun and providing a canvas for the passing play of light and shadow across their surfaces. On many islands, immaculate houses sweep outward, spreading in all directions under the protective shadow of the hilltop fortresses that were once bastions of the Crusaders. In remote mountain villages, stone farmhouses with tumble-down balconies overlook pebbled lanes just wide enough for donkeys to pass. Often, there is a startling contrast between city and country homes. In the island centers of Rhodes, Cyprus, and Crete, new homes—complete with all the amenities we expect of Western civilization—are the norm. In the more remote mountain villages, it is not unusual to find an entire family living in a one-room home with a freshly swept dirt floor, the only modern conveniences being electricity and running water.

Magnificent castles also abound in the Greek Isles. Venetian fortresses dominate towns on Anáfi, Astypalaia, Crete, and Halki, among other islands. From the thirteenth century onward, Venetian armies fortified numerous sites throughout the Greek Isles and founded new cities. On Crete,

ABOVE: **A house on Kárpathos demonstrates the importance of family identity.**

ABOVE: **The scenery of the Greek Isles is among the most diverse on the planet. Inland from the blue seas and peaceful harbors, olive groves and wildflower meadows thrive in the mild climate.**

they constructed massive city walls, enclosing narrow alleyways that led to piazzas, churches, and palaces. Like all visitors to the Greek Isles, the Venetians fell under the spell of the natural and manmade beauty of these islands. They called the lovely island of Zakinthos *fior di Levante*, or "flower of the Levant." In the sixteenth century, they abandoned their medieval towns to Suleiman the Magnificent, sultan of the Ottoman Empire. The churches that the Crusaders built throughout the islands were soon replaced by lavish mosques and Turkish baths.

Above all, it is the ancient monuments of the Greek Isles that exert a mysterious fascination on visitors. In Crete, the royal palace at Knossos, with its halls, rooms, and passages dating from 2500 B.C.E., remains steeped in myth. Its lively frescoes reveal their creators' whimsical nature and inscriptions serve as a striking reminder of how highly civilized the island's inhabitants were at a time when the rest of Europe was still prehistoric. On Delos, the ruins of the great sanctuary resonate with the power of ancient monuments, and with their permanence, both in the landscape and in the collective memory of the Greeks.

Land and Sea

The brilliant colors are the first thing that strike a visitor to the Greek Isles. From the stunning azure waters and blindingly white houses to the deep green-black of cypresses and the sky-blue domes of a thousand churches, saturated hues dominate the landscape. A strong, constant sun brings out all of nature's colors with great intensity.

Basking in sunshine, the Greek Isles enjoy a year-round temperate climate. Lemons grow to the size of grapefruits and grapes hang in heavy clusters from the vines of arbors that shade tables outside the tavernas. The silver leaves of olive trees shiver in the least sea breezes.

The Greek Isles boast some of the most spectacular and diverse geography on Earth. From natural hot springs to arcs of soft-sand beaches and secret valleys, the scenery is characterized by dramatic beauty. Volcanic formations send craggy cliffsides plummeting to the sea, cause lone rock formations to emerge from blue waters, and carve beaches of black pebbles. In the Valley of the Butterflies on Rhodes, thousands of radiant winged creatures blanket the sky in summer. Crete's Samaria Gorge is the longest in Europe, a magnificent natural wonder rife with local flora and fauna. Corfu bursts with lush greenery and wildflowers, nurtured by heavy rainfall and a sultry sun. The mountain ranges, gorges, and riverbeds on Andros recall the mainland more than the islands. Both golden beaches and rocky countrysides make Mykonos distinctive. Around Mount Olympus, in central Cyprus, timeless villages emerge from the morning mist of craggy peaks and scrub vegetation. On Evia and Ikaria, natural hot springs draw those seeking the therapeutic power of healing waters.

Caves abound in the Greek Isles; there are some three thousand on Crete alone. The Minoans gathered to worship their gods in the shallow caves that pepper the remotest hilltops and mountain ranges. A cave near the town of Amnissos, a shrine to Eileithyia, goddess of childbirth, once revealed a treasure trove of small idols dedicated to her. Some caves were later transformed into monasteries. On the islands of Halki and Cyprus, wall paintings on the interiors of such natural monasteries survive from the Middle Ages.

Above ground, trees and other flora abound on the islands in a stunning variety. On Crete, a veritable forest of palm trees shades the beaches at Vai and Preveli, while the high, desolate plateaus of the interior gleam in the sunlight. Forest meets sea on the island of Poros, and on Thasos, many species of pine coexist. Cedars, cypress, oak, and chestnut trees blanket the mountainous interiors of Crete, Cyprus, and other large islands. Rhodes overflows with wildflowers during the summer months.

Even a single island can be home to disparate natural wonders. Amorgos' steep, rocky coastline gives way to tranquil bays. The scenery of Crete—the largest of the Greek Isles—ranges from majestic mountains and barren plateaus to expansive coves, fertile valleys, and wooded thickets.

Some of the world's rarest creatures inhabit the Greek Isles. Monk seals, once found throughout the Mediterranean, still sun themselves on the coastal stretches of the Sporades in the Aegean. The shores along Alonyssos and the surrounding

islands have been made into a protected marine park for the once-endangered animals. The wild goat known as the *kri-kri* roams the craggy mountaintops of Crete. Sea turtles dally in the clear waters of Zakinthos, and lay their eggs on pristine beaches.

Against this backdrop of diverse geography, farming and fishing still dominate the economy. Many farmers rely on mule transportation and agricultural techniques that have persisted for generations. They tend citrus and olive groves planted by their forefathers, and cultivate grapes, figs, capers, olives, wheat, and tobacco. Family-run enterprises extract marble, pumice, and iron ore from local sources. The island of Halki derives its name from the Greek word for copper (*halkos*), a reminder of the copper mines that once covered it. Manufacturers on the island of Chios have long produced *mastichochoria*, an aromatic resin used to make cosmetics and employed in other industries as well.

These rocky, verdant, and volcanic landscapes of the Greek Isles exert their own charm, but it is the sea that dominates every aspect of life. Winding paths hug the shoreline,

ABOVE: **Wine barrels on Zakinthos decant fragrant, sweet wines fashioned by home vintners.**

revealing hidden coves and inlets of turquoise water sparkling in the sun. So many constructions—whether house, church, shop, or restaurant—offer a vista of the blue sea. Terraces spilling over with bougainvillea, and balconies bearing hand-hewn wooden chairs take advantage of the views afforded by crescent-shaped harbors and quiet bays. Each island takes pride in its own picturesque fishing harbors. Off the ports of Kalymnos, fishermen and skin divers gather sponges, octopi, grouper, and shellfish.

Some ten thousand years ago—perhaps even longer—people began to explore these enchanting seas. Cycladic pottery dating from 3000 B.C.E. depicts longboats powered by strong-backed oarsmen. The thousands of inviting islands—many in view of one another—must have made travel appealingly safe.

Archaeological evidence of ancient trade proves that the inhabitants of the Greek Isles knew their neighbors in Egypt, Assyria, and other parts of Asia Minor. The ancient Minoans traded with the Phoenicians, Syrians, and Egyptians as early as the third millennium B.C.E. The Greek Isles formed an important link between Europe and Asia, and experienced seafarers made interaction among these diverse cultures possible. The Greek islanders became renowned for commerce. Merchants from Thasos traded gold, silver, marble, and other luxury goods, traveling all over the Mediterranean. Rhodes became a major naval power from the fifth to the third century B.C.E., and was called the "Sovereign of the Seas" for its accomplishments in shipbuilding, sea travel, and military dominance of the oceans.

Intrepid sailors and fishermen navigating these heavily trafficked waters have recounted tall tales and formulated popular wisdom that persists to the present day. According to ancient inscriptions, sailors always docked their ships at Delos when the rugged peaks

ABOVE: **Off Corfu, vestiges of ancient Greek civilization linger beneath blue waters. Naval archaeologists have uncovered important information about earlier times in the waters of the Greek Isles.**

of the island of Tinos were covered in clouds, for this atmospheric condition nearly always presaged a storm. Today's boatmen still gaze toward Tinos to gauge the weather before launching their craft.

Though their purpose may have changed from trade and fishing to the pursuit of pleasure, seagoing vessels still grace the blue seas with bright colors laden with tradition. Homer's *Odyssey* offers a glimpse of boat building in antiquity, and shipwrecks throughout the Greek Isles confirm that modern boats are not too far removed from their ancient predecessors. In the historic boatyard on Spetsi, craftsmen have been making wooden boats according to centuries-old methods. Today, Andros is home to many Greek seamen and has a flourishing boat-building industry that remains an important part of the economy of the Greek Isles.

Nevertheless, it is the small towns and villages along the shores that form the economic and cultural base of the Greek Isles. From the larger centers of Rhodes and Crete to the tiny settlements of a thousand islets, daily life often continues at a pace that appears nearly unchanged by time and technology. Approaching from the sea gives the visitor a true feel for the individual beauty of each village. On Halki, the buildings of the main town are arrayed around the crystal-clear waters of the small port like bleachers in an amphitheater. On Folegandros, the houses themselves form a retaining wall around the harbor town. Zakinthos boasts arcaded streets, shaded squares, and neat houses facing the port.

ABOVE: **Tomatoes and figs dry under the strong sun on the island of Anafi.**

In each portside town, enticing aromas waft from every harborside taverna, mountaintop inn, and home. Not only do the Greeks appreciate good food, it is central to their culture. Produce markets spill over with fragrant local provender: grapes, cucumbers, lemons, and tomatoes, as well as sardines, shellfish, and lamb. Lunch—usually the largest meal of the day—begins after 2 P.M., and is followed by an ample siesta. The long work day resumes, and dinner begins after 9 P.M. It may last well into the night among friends: a glass of ouzo—accompanied by singing, guitar playing, and dancing—often ends the evening meal, postponing bedtime until the wee hours. Laughter and conversation flavor the food at every meal.

The Mediterranean climate is conducive to year-round outdoor eating. In each home, a table on the patio or terrace takes pride of place. Many home cooks build outdoor ovens and prepare succulent roasted meats and flavorful, herb-scented potatoes that soak up the juice of the meat and the spritz of a lemon. Tavernas, shaded by grape arbors, are synonymous with Greece and its outdoor culinary culture. One of the greatest pleasures of the Greek Isles is enjoying a relaxing meal while breathing the fresh sea air and gazing out on spectacular vistas and blue waters.

Meals are occasions to share with family and friends. The ingredients are often simple, but the art lies in orchestrating the sun-warmed flavors. Courses follow in artful and traditional succession, but the showpiece of the meal is tender, juicy meat; this often means lamb or goat grilled or roasted on a spit for hours. Souvlaki—melting pieces of chicken or pork tenderloin on skewers, marinated in lemon, olive oil, and a blend of seasonings—are grilled to mouthwatering perfection. *Meze*, the Greek version of smorgasbord, is a feast of Mediterranean delicacies.

The cooks of the Greek Isles excel at classic Greek fare, such as *spanakopita*—delicate phyllo dough brushed with butter and filled with layers of feta cheese, spinach, and herbs. Cheeses made from goat's milk, including the famous feta, are nearly ubiquitous. The fruits of the sun—olive oil and lemon—are characteristic flavors, reworked in myriad wonderful combinations. The fresh, simple cuisine celebrates the waters, olive groves, and citrus trees, as well as the herbs that

ABOVE: **Fig pie is a specialty of Corfu. The figs are painstakingly wrapped in leaves and tied with string.**

grow wild all over the islands—marjoram, thyme, and rose-mary—scenting the warm air with their sensuous aromas.

Not surprisingly, of course, seafood holds pride of place. Sardines, octopus, and squid, marinated in olive oil and lemon juice, are always popular. Tiny, toothsome fried fish are piled high on painted ceramic dishes and served up at the local tavernas and in homes everywhere. Sea urchins are considered special delicacies.

Every island has its own specialties, from sardines to pistachios to sesame cakes. Lésvos is well-known for its sardines and ouzo. Zakinthos is famous for its nougat. The Cycladic island of Astypalaia was called the "paradise of the gods" by the ancient Greeks because of the quality of its honey. On weekends, Athenians flock to the nearby islands of Aegina, Angistri, and Evia by the ferryful to sample the daily catch in local restaurants scattered among coastal villages.

The array of culinary treats is matched by a similar breadth of local wines. Tended by generation after generation of the same families, vineyards carpet the hillsides of many islands. Grapevines have been cultivated in the Greek Isles for some four thousand years. Wines from Rhodes and Crete were already renowned in antiquity, and traders shipped them throughout the Greek Isles and beyond. The light reds and gently sweet whites complement the diverse, multiflavored Greek seafood, grilled meats, and fresh, ripe fruits and vegetables. Sitting at a seaside taverna enjoying music and conversation over a midday meze and glass of *retsina*, all the cares in the world seem to evaporate in the sparkling sunshine reflected off the brightly hued boats and glistening blue waters.

A Vibrant Heritage

Today, ferries and sailboats—modern descendants of ancient sailing ships and fishing vessels—shuttle visitors from port to port throughout this vast chain of sun-soaked islands. Stepping ashore, the visitor is instantly enveloped by a way of life that is both utterly contemporary and ageless. The timeless tang of the sea, the calls of fisherman and market women, the deep, complex fragrance of wild rosemary form a seamless whole with the sheep that graze in the shadow of windmills and fortresses, and the enduring ruins of ancient temples and baths: past and present are one.

The Greek Isles reflect the complex of cultures that have passed through them. In the island capital of Corfu for example, buildings reveal classical, Byzantine, Venetian, Turkish, and French influences. To fully appreciate the present, you must peel back layers of time. Minoan palaces gave way to ancient temples and Roman villas, then to Byzantine churches and fortresses. Venetian fortresses were raised on Byzantine foundations. Turkish invaders added their own monuments. The Church of Our Lady of the Castle on Rhodes began as a Byzantine church, was transformed by Genoese Crusaders into a Roman Catholic church, then became a mosque in the sixteenth century. Now, it is a church once more. Modern "improvements" are not always useful in the rugged topography of the islands: on many islands, such as Hydra, not a car is to be found; people travel by donkey or on foot.

The radiant sun draws visitors from the cold climes of Scandinavia, Britain, and Germany, and lively tavernas and

discotheques entice vacationers from Asia and the Americas. People come from all over the world to marvel at the breathtaking historical depth and breadth that greets the visitor at every turn. This very mix of nationalities is just the latest of the many waves that have washed upon the Greek Isles for millennia. As they have since ancient, seafaring times, the hospitable inhabitants of the Greek Isles welcome these strangers who come for the beaches and the antiquities—and leave with the gift of the joy of living.

As sunset gives way to the blanket of night, the modest lights of a thousand tiny villages twinkle and flicker as if mirroring the star-studded sky. Against the darkness, the columns and stones of ancient temples and theaters glow with a secret whiteness. Sipping a sweet and aromatic coffee, as a mandolin player strums an ancient melody and waves lap up against fishing boats moored for the night, it is easy to understand why the ancients believed these magical islands to be the birthplace of the gods.

ABOVE: **Thousands of tiny islets—many of them virtually uninhabited—dot the Aegean, Ionian, and Mediterranean seas. Ancient ruins, lone chapels, and historic lighthouses draw visitors to the otherwise barren landscapes of these intriguing locales.**

PART II

IMAGES

PAGES 32–33: **Appearing like a miniature paradise on earth, a private cove on Zakinthos welcomes visitors arriving by boat from the azure waters lapping its white shores.**

LEFT: **On the island of Milos, a corrugated cliffside plummets to the sea.**

ABOVE: **For millennia, crystal waters have carved beautiful patterns and shapes into the porous rock of the Greek Isles. On Corfu, striking rock formations create a secluded cove.**

✻

ABOVE: **On Lemnos, in the northeast Aegean Sea, these rock formations have been so sculpted by wind and sea that they resemble giant mounds of whipped cream.**

RIGHT: **Crete boasts some of the most various scenery of the Greek Isles. At Iráklion, craggy hillsides appear striped in the bright sun.**

LEFT: **A drift of prickly pears, bearing thirst-quenching fruit, tumbles down a steep slope.**

ABOVE: **The church of Agios Constantinos—Saint Constantine— stands on a rocky hillside on the island of Serifos. The faithful climb many steps to reach the immaculate white church at the top of the hill.**

ABOVE: Worn by sun and time, the church of Agios Nicolaos—Saint Nicholas, a patron saint of sailors—seems to rise from
the very soil of the island of Skíros, in the Sporades.

ABOVE: The shores of Chios have witnessed thousands of years of history. During the third and second centuries B.C.E., some of the Greek Isles developed cultural centers important enough to compete with mainland Athens.

ABOVE: **A ruined windmill—long since abandoned—stands in silhouette on a windswept plain in the Cyclades.**

ABOVE: **Overlooking a deep blue sea, the monastery of Panagia**

Chozoviotissa on Amórgos clings to the cliffside.

Christian monks founded paradisical retreats in monasteries

throughout the Greek Isles.

ABOVE: **In the rocky, mountainous landscape of many Greek Isles, farmers have cultivated olive trees, grapevines, and other crops for centuries. Few parcels of land are left untilled.**

ABOVE: **The Greek Isles present some of the most otherworldly landscapes on earth. On Serifos, the earth forms ruddy terraces,**
which seem to plummet into the sea.

ABOVE: Grapes hang in heavy bunches in the fields of one of Crete's famous wineries.

ABOVE: **On Crete's hillsides, decades-old olive trees carpet the landscape and traditional olive presses like this one stand ready to turn the rich fruit into full-bodied oil, prized the world over.**

PAGES 48–49: **In a harbor of Mykonos, freshly painted boats bob in peaceful waters. Welcoming tavernas and family-owned shops greet visitors to this magical island.**

OPPOSITE: **A lone chapel presides over a quiet harbor on Mykonos. The simple, sometimes even severe exterior of many Greek churches belies a sumptuous interior of golden icons glittering in flickering candlelight.**

ABOVE: **An Orthodox priest makes his way among the scrubby vegetation on inland Kárpathos.**

LEFT: **On Kárpathos, villagers have retained their ancentral ways into the twenty-first century. Traditional architecture, dress, language, and customs prevail.**

BELOW: **A study in form and color, a church on the island of Kárpathos reflects the Mediterranean sun.**

ABOVE: **On Mykonos, a red door contrasts with the white stucco of this Greek Orthodox church.**

RIGHT: **A picture-perfect harbor in Mykonos shelters a nesting flock of sailboats.**

ABOVE: **A priest on Serifos surveys the view from his hilltop church.**

ABOVE: **Bright red, blue, and white contrast to make a stunning display of the church of Triada, on Serifos.**

LEFT: **On Crete, Preveli Monastery carries on ancient monastic traditions. For nearly two thousand years, religious communities have made their homes in the Greek Isles.**

ABOVE: **Samos boasts a postcard-pretty, crescent-shaped harbor filled with bobbing masts and fishing boats.**

LEFT: **Sunset on Santorini is famous, drawing visitors from around the globe to bask in its gilded glow.**

ABOVE: **Nightfall brings celebrations in the Greek Isles. Against a burning sunset, pristine white towns and deep blue harbors are spangled with twinkling lights and alive with music, dancing, and laughter.**

OPPOSITE: **On Rhodes, medieval architects combined Western building techniques with an Eastern spirit. The result is some of the most fanciful, colorful architecture found anywhere in the Mediterranean.**

RIGHT: **The striking white dome of Panagia Kalamiotissa church, on Anafi, overlooks a blue sky and sea.**

✳

LEFT: The almost organic lines of the architecture of the Greek Isles offer stunning contrasts and aesthetic moments, like this one in the village of Artemonas, on Sifnós.

ABOVE: **Narrow paths wander among homes and churches above a turquoise sea.**

OPPOSITE: **On Paros, in the Cyclades, a blue-domed church seems to exert a protective force over an island village.**

ABOVE: **Many Greek Orthodox churches incorporate three principal shapes—a circle, octagon, and a cross with four equal arms. A dome is always the prominent feature of this architecture. Small windows below the dome admit an ethereal, awe-inspiring light into the cool penumbra of the interior.**

LEFT: **Bright colors, geometric forms, and occasional playful details characterize the architecture of the Greek Isles. This house on Corfu embodies the understated whimsy of the Greek spirit.**

OPPOSITE: **Reflecting the azure waters, this house on Kalymnos exerts a striking allure. In the Greek Isles, even the most utilitarian structure is a feast for the eyes.**

LEFT: The Greek Isles are composed of thousands of rocky islets like these, off the coast of Zakinthos. These uninhabited crags of land can be reached only by boat.

ABOVE: Traditions run deep in the Greek Isles, as this woman's clothing proves. In the isolated mountain village of Olympos, on Kárpathos, people still use some ancient Greek words.

ABOVE: **A prosperous homeowner on Patmos displays the objects of her history: old photographs, lace, local handicrafts, and antique furniture.**

LEFT: **To many Greek islanders, it is important to instill traditional values and pass on the local customs to the next generation. Children learn the ways of their ancestors through language, dress, and cultural events.**

ABOVE: These bronze doors recall the era of the seagoing Venetians, who ruled many Greek islands
from the thirteenth to the sixteenth century, and who left their mark
through fortified castles and new cities.

RIGHT: Arkadi Monastery houses glittering icons and centuries of tradition
behind its still imposing facade.

LEFT: **At a wedding ceremony in the village of Olympos, on Kárpathos, the wedding party wears richly embroidered clothing.**

ABOVE: **Mesanagros Church on Rhodes displays colorful religious icons, some of which are only brought out on feast days.**

LEFT: **Whether ancient paganism or Orthodox Christianity, spirituality and religion have always played a profound role in the culture of the Greek Isles.**

OPPOSITE: **On Lemnos, two icons stand vigil in a streetside chapel. Local worshippers stop by with offerings of flowers and prayers.**

ABOVE: **Greek texts were preserved and copied for centuries in the monasteries of the Greek Isles. At Evangelistria Monastery on Skiathos, the library is a treasure trove of early Christian writings.**

RIGHT: **According to Orthodox ritual, priests perform parts of the service behind the *templon*, or screen, here decorated with brightly colored panel paintings and icons.**

ABOVE: **Off the coast of Crete, beautiful, idyllic Spinalonga shelters a somber past: the islet once housed a leper colony.**

RIGHT: **According to legend, it was here on Naxos, largest of the Cyclades, that Theseus abandoned Ariadne, the princess who enabled him to escape the Minotaur's Labyrinth. The ruins of an unfinished temple to Apollo rise, overlooking the Aegean.**

OPPOSITE: **On Chios, tomatoes dry in the warm air. From honey to sardines to pistachios, each Greek island boasts its own culinary specialty.**

ABOVE: **Myth and history converge in the Greek Isles. At Panagia Chozoviotissa Monastery on Amorgos, an ancient vessel is silhouetted in the reflected light. In the Cyclades, inhabitants have worshipped in caverns and cliffsides caves for thousands of years.**

OPPOSITE: **Traditional handicrafts flourish in the Greek Isles. On Kimolos, a craftsman creates a woven ceiling for a local home. Traditional crafts are kept in the family and passed down through the generations.**

RIGHT: **A modest, timeless still life is composed of a few elements: a wreath and a market scale.**

LEFT: **At an antique shop on Astypalaia, a sculpted angel prays to a cerulean sky.**

OPPOSITE: **Strong, brilliant hues—here, blues, reds, and greens—harmonize against spotless white, in the light of the Mediterranean sun.**

ABOVE: **The sunsets on the tranquil waters of the seaside town of Venetia, on Mykonos offer a glimpse of eternity.**

PAGE 96: **Colorful boats are ubiquitous in the Cyclades, where they are easily spotted offshore. Ancient shipwrecks—only recently explored by archaeologists—demonstrate that modern craft are not far removed from those of more than two thousand years ago.**

INDEX

Pea Pod Lullaby

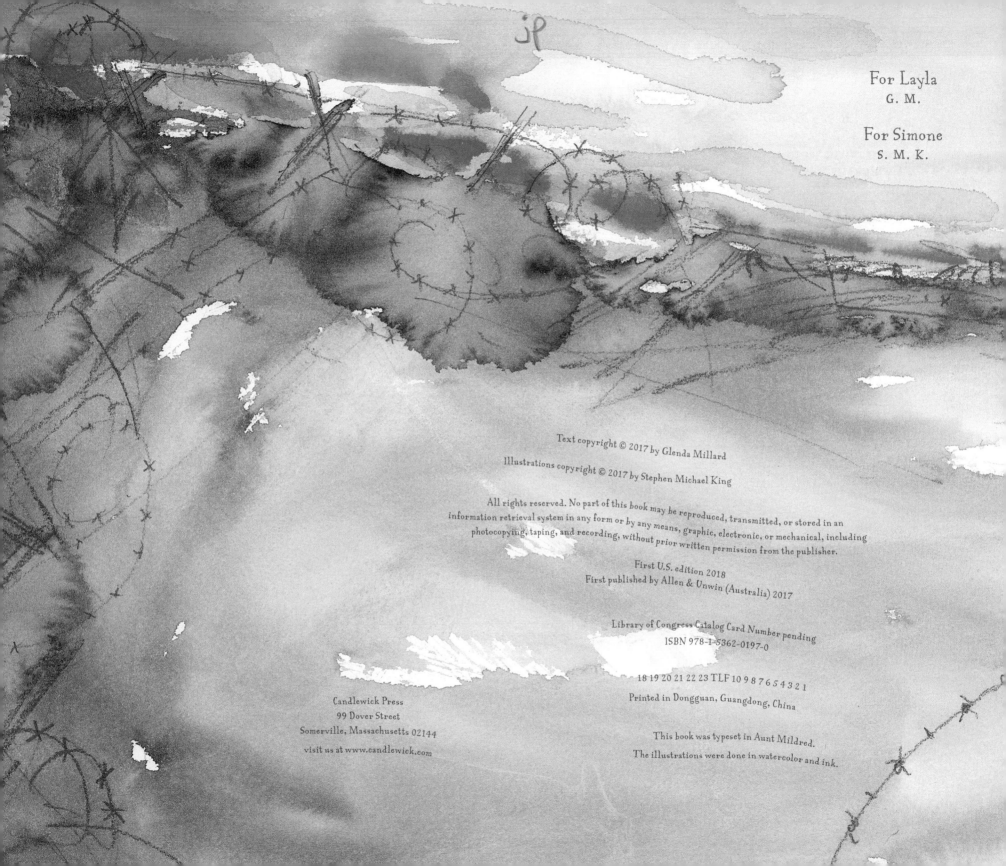

For Layla
G. M.

For Simone
S. M. K.

First U.S. edition 2018
First published by Allen & Unwin (Australia) 2017

Library of Congress Catalog Card Number pending
ISBN 978-1-5362-0197-0

18 19 20 21 22 23 TLF 10 9 8 7 6 5 4 3 2 1

Printed in Dongguan, Guangdong, China

This book was typeset in Aunt Mildred.
The illustrations were done in watercolor and ink.

Candlewick Press
99 Dover Street
Somerville, Massachusetts 02144

visit us at www.candlewick.com

GLENDA MILLARD

illustrated by
STEPHEN MICHAEL KING

Pea Pod
Lullaby

CANDLEWICK PRESS

I am the small green pea

you are the tender pod

hold me

I am the diving kite

you are the bow-tied tail

steady me

I am the drifting boat

you are the quiet deep

buoy me

I am the fleeting breath

you are the universe

shelter me

I am the falling star

you are the wishful hands

catch me

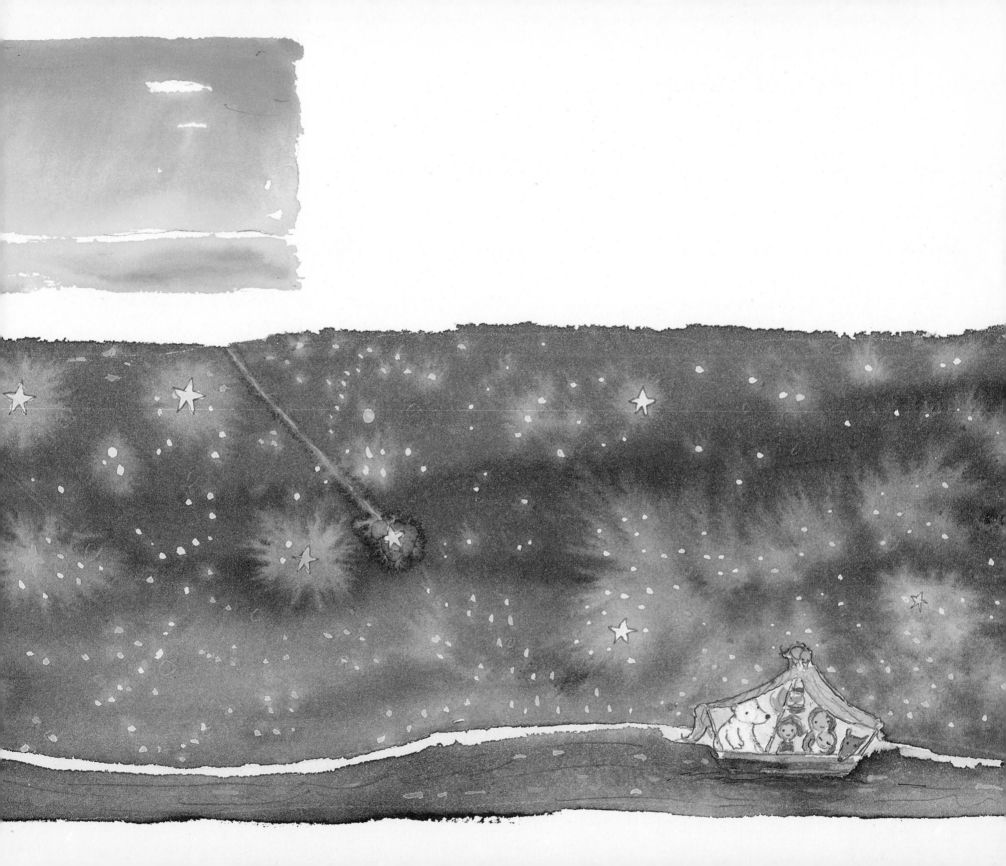

I am the windblown husk

you are the jeweled rain

quench me

I am the sapphire night

you are the lantern moon

light me

I am the looking glass

you are the image there

see me

I am the tumbling leaf

you are the whispered breeze

dance me

I am the castaway

you are the journey's end

welcome me

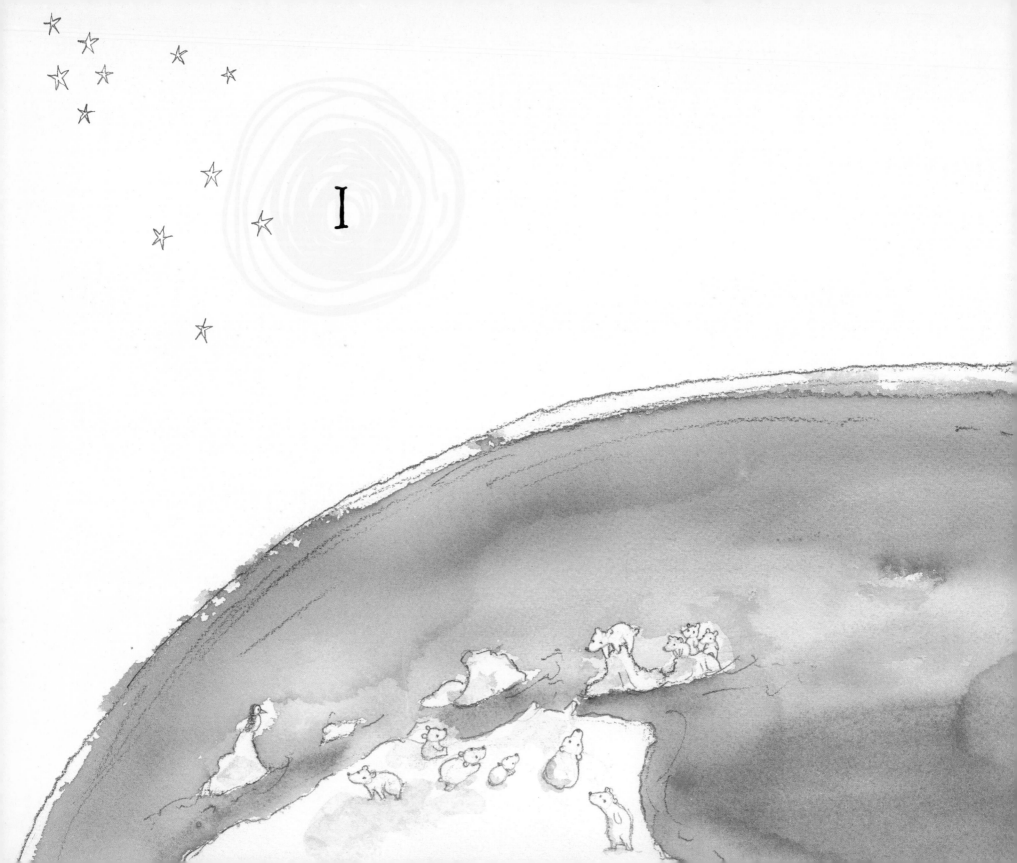

I

You

We

For Glenda Millard and Stephen Michael King, the making of *Pea Pod Lullaby* was a particularly special experience. Glenda joined Stephen at the Manning Regional Art Gallery in Taree, New South Wales, Australia, where Stephen was creating the initial illustrations for the book as part of the gallery's Wall Project. As Stephen drew the scenes, Glenda placed the verses, revising the words as the storyboard emerged. They made the book together, trusting each other with their newly formed ideas and welcoming the comments of people in the gallery who watched the author and illustrator at work.